WE BECAME AS MOUNTAINS

WE BECAME
AS MOUNTAINS

POEMS OF THE SPANISH CONQUEST

NANCY WOOD

WESTERN EDGE PRESS, Santa Fe

ISBN: 1-889921-22-X
ISBN 13: 978-1-889921-22-8

Library of Congress Control Number: 2008932163

Cover image by Frank Howell.
The Passage, 1981, Stone lithograph. Courtesy of Dan Howell.

Cover and text design by Jim Mafchir

Western Edge Press
126 Candelario St.
Santa Fe, NM 87501
westernedge@santa-fe.net
www.westernedgepress.com

Printed in Canada

Contents

For Bob and Prue
with thanks

The author wishes to thank Foxhole Parker, Dave Willsey,
and Jim Mafchir for their help and support

The earth was created by the assistance of the sun, and it should be left as it was. The country was made without lines of demarcation and it is no man's business to divide it.

Chief Joseph

Today almost all the prophecies have come to pass. Great roads like rivers pass along the landscape; man talks to man through the cobwebs of telephone lines; man travels along the roads in the sky in his airplanes; two great wars have been waged by those bearing the swastika or the rising sun; man is tampering with the Moon and the stars. Most men have strayed from the path shown us by the Great Spirit. For Massau'u alone is great enough to portray the way back to him.

Thomas Banyacya, Hopi elder

Preface

Each time I walk the tawny grass around my house, I see the rough contours of New Mexico history. Where are the dinosaurs that thudded along when my land was a lush, green swamp? No people then, just deafening noise and monsters eating trees. Time passed. Millions of years of gradual change. And then.

Indians camped here, hunted in nearby mountains, passed on their knowledge to their children. They observed the seasons, the land around them, animals and birds. Gods came down from the sky and told them how to live. Lessons expanded until death, and then continued. Knowledge was cumulative.

Pottery shards and arrow chips are scattered over the ground. I pick them up and hold them in my hand. Where is the woman who made this pot, the man who carved an arrowhead? My Indian friends say they are still around. Just look.

I stand at the base of a sandstone cliff and stare at petroglyphs of a bighorn sheep, a humpbacked flute player, an elk. They were made a thousand years ago. I feel the wind, hear something stirring in the junipers. I am not alone. The conquistadores might ride up at any moment, banners flying, bringing God and destruction to the Indians. I can almost hear their Castilian voices, the soft breathing of the horses. How must the Pueblos have felt when they saw them coming? They threw themselves at their feet, thinking they were gods. The illusion did not last long.

The poems in this book tell a brutal story, but I have another story, too.

Where they came from

In 1540, the conquistadores rode north from Mexico where they had wiped out the Aztec civilization. It was the Spanish Inquisition. Bloodthirsty, not much inclined to respect others different from themselves, the conquistadores rode with an imperious air, the friars following on foot. The Spaniards sought gold; the friars sought converts to Catholicism. For each converted heathen they received clerical points. The Pueblos resisted and were murdered by the thousands.

The genocide of the North American Indian population began in sixteenth-century New Mexico when life as Indians knew it came to an end.

Life under the Conquistadores

Genocide makes one think of the Nazi annihilation of six million Jews, murdered because they were different. The

Indians on the North American continent were different, too: five hundred tribes with different languages, stories, customs, and traditional beliefs.

For a century after the Spanish incursion, the Pueblos fought for their lives. They felt the sharp sting of their masters' whips; they burned at the stake, beheaded, starved, and tortured. More than one hundred Pueblos were annihilated, women and children included. Many succumbed to disease such as small pox; others were murdered when they refused to accept Catholicism. Why not listen to a bear, a blue jay, the song of rain? they said. God is in these things.

Blasphemy, said the Spaniards. Try telling a priest that God is in rain. Or that Indians can become a mountain to escape danger. Indian men were forced to guide the Spaniards to nonexistent deposits of gold. They were dragged up into the mountains to carry back down heavy timbers with which to build churches. Many died from exhaustion. Others starved when the Spaniards requisitioned their food. They should have been exterminated, a mere footnote to history by now. They went on.

Transition

The Pueblos are quiet now, though the kivas, the centers of native religion, are active with boys and men participating in ancient rituals. White men who pry into them are known to be beaten ... or worse. Something holy and enduring arises from the smoke-filled villages, no matter how much the modern world intrudes. The Indians attend Sunday mass and celebrate Catholic feast days, but it is their own faith that prevails as it has from the Beginning Time when animals became people.

There are no plaster saints in the Pueblo religion, only kachinas, or doll-like figures, who guide every waking moment of their lives. Behind thick Pueblo walls, more than six hundred years old, a drumbeat rises, soft at first, then louder and louder. A throbbing spirituality prevails. When I walk around the plaza, it's as though I'm handling the thread that spun out from the eyes of time. If I close my eyes I can see small red men skinning a deer, women grinding corn, children running after dogs. I can create my own past whenever I want to escape the world.

Today and Beyond

The Pueblos are thriving economically with lucrative casinos on every reservation, each more lavish than the one before. In a strange irony, the Spaniards and Anglos work for the Indian now as hotels, Indian-owned shopping centers, and businesses have sprung up. Money is rolling in, yet many of the old habits survive—not only good ones. Women, for instance, do not vote in tribal elections. It's time they did, but the patriarchal councils refuse to give them the right. Homes are modest, usually BIA pre-fabs. Cornfields have long been abandoned; food is bought in the supermarket.

Every August 10, I commemorate the Pueblo Revolt of 1680 when the Pueblos murdered the priests and drove the Spaniards out. I rejoice over this great act of rebellion that took place from Taos to Zuni, a distance of over 200 rugged miles. Impossible—yet they did it. I celebrate the Indian victory with like-minded sentimentalists. We would not want to be living back then with small pox running rampant, food scarce, and filthy water. We like the idea of freedom it represents, though. If we could overthrow our current government, it would be a good thing, too.

I wrote this narrative poem to make a record of dreams and what passes for progress. I haven't tried for historical perfection, rather for a sensory perception of what might have been and what actually was. Or maybe never was. Who knows?

Nancy Wood
Santa Fe, New Mexico

THE BEGINNING TIME

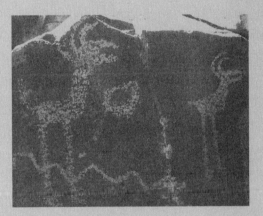

TODAY AND YESTERDAY

Today is yesterday
and yesterday is today.
Tomorrow is a return to
a life that vanished long ago.

I feel it in my bones, me a modern man
living in a modern house. I'm old, like
buffalo warriors are old, like my grandfather was
old even before he was born. I see eagles

When they had room to fly and deer were unconfined
by fences. I see the war councils we used to have
and the killing of the deer by the bravest man.
One arrow was all he was allowed.

Now I watch television, eat pizza,
and play baseball in the plaza.
I'm a modern Indian, except when
I go into the mountains and sit on a log,
waiting for my ancestors to come rushing in.

ORIGINS

This is the way it was before the world took shape.

The Old Man and the Old Woman
were invisible
except to the eyes that had created them
out of dust and fire and stars.

When the Old Man discovered
the Old Woman sleeping
beneath the blanket of the Milky Way,
he recognized
the potential between them. She had soft energy,

While his was hard and relentless. A cloud
of mystery surrounded her, though he found her
to be perplexing. She didn't speak to him for ages,
even when he offered sustenance. She refused
when he suggested they connect
across the abyss. I desire more,
she said. The Old Man wondered what it was.

The Old Woman recognized in him
the ability to become useful,
also a willingness
to make decisions. She admired his plans
for the future, but he lacked tenderness

and what she perceived
as flexibility. He chased her across
infinity, trying to melt her resistance.

Eventually, the Old Woman heard
what she had desired all that time.
I love you,
he said. The Old Woman said
she loved him too.

When they came together,
the fire of creation burst
across the Void and filled it
with Potential.
Everything necessary for creation
was there, going round and round.

CONNECTIONS

Life began in harmony. The winged creatures
and the fish,
the mystery of eggs,
the fragility of anemones.

Sun and moon were allies, also crickets
and rattlesnakes, each thing
connected to another.

The Old Woman's mystery
and the Old Man's predictability
       made corn
       and clay
       and bones
essential to the beginning of life.

When all was in order, the Old Woman
and the Old Man went away.
       Our work is finished, they said.

CREATION SONG

The first sounds of the universe were footsteps,
    though human beings were not alive.
The footsteps went from star to star, wearing
    a pathway of potential through the sky.

They gave away desire, which precedes
    a heartbeat waiting to be born.
The first songs arose
    from nothingness.

Sacred voices said: We are wing and bone,
    blood and skin. We are what
    will never die. That was all
    the earth needed in order to awaken.

The footsteps went on,
    and inside the mystery of creation,
    they gave the power of connection
    to creatures emerging
    from the womb.

BEGINNING TIME

In the Beginning Time was stillness.
No color and no music.
No flowers and no rain.

In the Beginning Time, our Great-grandmother
was a Void called Wisdom,
the Original Emptiness.

In the Beginning Time, our Great-grandfather
was the Milky Way,
a Long Sash of Potential.

This was the first universal truth, endless.

Then the sacred marriage of our Great-grandfather
        and Great-grandmother took place.
        She opened the Void and let him in.
        He placed Potential inside Wisdom, where it
        belonged.

This was the first universal mating, endless.

Our Great-grandparents made two children:
        First came Sun, breathing Fire and
        the Song of Illumination. Earth came next,
        offering her Deep Womb and

the Song of Unending Fruition.
The Spirits of Power and Forgiveness arose.

This was the second universal mating, endless.

These were our Grandparents. Then the sacred marriage
        of Earth and Sun took place,
        holy and unforgettable,
        blessed by Wisdom, Potential, Illumination,
        Fruition, and the Spirits of Power and Forgiveness.

This was the third universal mating, endless.

Our Grandparents made three children.
        Plants came first, bringing Medicine
        and the Song of Growing Things.
        Animals came second, bringing Food
        and the Song of Connected Knowledge.
        Humans came third, bringing Perception
        and the Song of Enlightened Beings.

These were the Ancestors, holy and unforgettable.

The sacred marriage of Plants, Animals, and Humans
        took place,
        blessed by Wisdom, Potential,
        Energy, Food, Perception,
        Illumination, Fruition, and the Spirits
        of Power and Forgiveness.

This was the fourth universal mating, which gave rise
to dreams, endless.

Dreams gave rise to sacred law, endless.
Sacred law gave rise to sacred motion, endless.
Sacred motion leads to the Original Emptiness, endless.
Out of the Original Emptiness, we became.

So it was for more time than could be measured.
And then people stirred and argued.
They began to want riches.

Countries fell.
False warriors emerged.
It was the end of harmony.

It was

       The end of Harmony
       The end of Potential
       The end of Illumination
       The end of the Original Emptiness

All over the world
people began to figure things out,
some weak, some strong.

Some traveled down rivers and

across oceans, up mountains
and down the other side.

The people spread out like birds.
They learned to walk like deer.

CHANGE

The Creator brought the people to a certain place
and set them down. They were only as big
as a thumb but they grew tall.

Everything good was to be found there. Game.
Water. Nuts. Berries. Red earth and blue sky.
Warriors to talk to. Beautiful women to marry.

And then the elders noticed strange creatures
coming out of the ground
and bats hanging right side up and birds
destroying their nests. The elders went to a hill

And looked down. Nothing except the river.
They sang and fasted for seven days. They beat
A blackened drum with its worldwide heartbeat.

What can it be? they asked. And waited.

FALL OF A GREAT PEOPLE

TENOCHTITLAN: 1521

Spain was moving.
Like an uncoiled snake it moved, slowly
devouring, hungry for possession,
for dominance,
for submission to Jesucristo and the holy rights of Kings.

The arrogant Son of Italy,
Admiral of Castile, embraced the Ptolemaic earth and
announced he had discovered
India's rich bounty rising from the sea.
In his frenzy he created new bloodlines, created slavery,
created misery among the innocents. So began
the downward spiral
toward obedience,
toward a strange religion,
toward oblivion.

Stone jaguars and war gods screamed,
macaws spoke in strange voices,
and whales became
messengers of destruction.
Los Indios fretted about their unborn children,
about rain-giving Tlaloc, about how
Huitzilopochtli would be remembered
as he fell face-down in the jungle.

Saturated in despair
were the jungles, the high mountains,
and death-scented shores
where human blood
mixed with sea water. It is finished, the Aztecs said,
and they smashed their holy relics
and tore their hair.

The future had already been determined
when Quetzacoatl's prophecy was fulfilled
in the year One Reed,
the year Tenochtitlan fell
and the spirits of mutilated Aztecs
went into the ground for safekeeping.
In the Valley of Mexico, monkeys became human,
palm trees turned upside down,
volcanoes stirred,
and across the perfumed land,
a bitterness arose.

Eyes upward, warriors released their fables
to the wind, while in ruined Tenochtitlan,
enormous war dogs,
whose eyes flashed fire,
looked northward,
hungrily.

THE ANIMAL BEINGS: 1540

After the Bat God shattered in Tenochtitlan,
      Tortoise set out on a slow journey
to warn his relatives about what was happening.
It took nearly twenty summers to get anywhere.

Macaw came too, and fearless Jaguar,
running around the stinking corpses
      and the ruined palaces
      and the darkness
      that swallowed up the sun.

The world is ending, Macaw chirped,
but no one believed him.
The world is ending, said Tortoise.
Leave quickly, Jaguar said,
but the people dozed in the sun.

Something dreadful is coming, said the Monkey
with a golden cup, traveling on two legs.
Listen to what I tell you.
The people threw him a nut. Be still, they said.

The men were scraping hides.
The women were making flat bread on a hot rock.
The children played a game with stones.

The sun shone down with its life-giving goodness.
Ah, the elders said, you animals are crazy.

Then a lookout came running in.
The gods have come, he said. They ride
great animals and they are covered in shiny
cloth. They mean no harm. Come and see,
you learned ones.

Macaw, Jaguar, and Tortoise pressed against a wall
waiting to see what happened next.

THE CONQUEST OF NEW SPAIN

The long column of homesick soldiers
rode toward Hawikuh,
wearing heavy metal suits in the sweltering sun,
flying the twin banners of God and country,
with an unstable general named Coronado
riding at the head.

He saw the Seven Cities of Gold
just over the hill shimmering in the sunlight,
and he ordered haste
before the mirage disappeared.
The conquistadores began to whisper
of the madness of their leader, but they rode on
toward imaginary gold, toward conquest.

The people of Hawikuh saw them coming
across the parched sand, and they wondered
why the ravens formed an arrow in the sky.
What are these magnificent beasts big enough for
a man to ride? Come, we will greet them.
We are glad to welcome strangers.
The elders donned their furs and feathers
and opened their arms in greeting.

St. James and at them! cried the general
and spurred his horse. The arquebuses fired

and the soldiers surged forward, bearing down on people
who fell to the earth, dead.

Monkey ran to the rooftop
and shouted to those who survived. Macaw flew
off to a tree and tore his feathers out. Jaguar retreated
into the hills
and waited for life to change.

As for Tortoise, he lived inside his shell from then on.

The general raised a flask of water to his lips.
The conquest of New Spain had begun.

HAWIKUH: 1540 ~ FRAY JUAN CARLOS

Heathens,
        I called them, savages
worshipping dead animals, naked
            as babies, treacherous as snakes,
            looking at me with erotic defiance.

While the Knight of the Plains begged
            those beggars of Hawikuh
            for allegiance to Nuestro Rey Magnifico,
I urged them to embrace Nuestro Padre Jesus.
            Gloria Patri, et Filio, et Spiritu Sanctu.

        Pater Noster must be obeyed.

Pagans soon to become Christians,
I addressed them as they fell to their knees
            to kiss the holy crucifix, repulsed
            at how they rubbed against our horses and
            pushed their bare-breasted women toward us.

Niños de Dios, I implored, pobrecitos, as the holy water
            of baptism failed to cleanse
            their sinfulness. They,
            being weak of mind and spirit, licked
            the droplets with coarse tongues,
            then laughed at me. Madre de Dios!

Pater Noster must be obeyed.

Those wretched pagans of Hawikuh
        Ketchipauan
        Kwakina
        Halona
        Matsaki
        Kwakina

Lived in sin, in filth, in licentiousness,
        pretending to embrace
        Pater Noster,
        La Madre de Dios,
        Nuestro Rey Magnifico.

But I, having gorged myself on God,
        knew better.

Orate fratres, I prayed. Dust answered me,
        and scorpions, and dry lizards
with forked tongues. The general crossed the
        cornmeal line
        put there to deter us from our mission. He said:
        We come in peace, but the jefes must recognize
                authority.
                Por Dios
                Por Nuestra Madre España.

Our weapons must be obeyed.

The arquebuses and the crossbows
>   connected with the wretches. The village
>   crumbled
>   and the people ran out with their dead babies,
>   begging for mercy.

Dogs, the general said and raised his sword above his head.
Blood ran like water across the plaza. White clouds fell.
>   Jesucristo saves sinners.
>   Deo gratias. Amen.

WHEN MEMORY DIES, ARENAL: 1580

When memory dies, the purpose of a people is obliterated.

Long ago at Arenal, earth and sky were mysteries,
        joined at the heart, male to female,
        inseparable. Elders honored the lessons
        of seasons, the kinship of snakes
        with birds, and the power of bears who
        were once human grandfathers.

No one revealed sacred knowledge
        for it was the blood of life to them.
People sang the same songs
        for a thousand years and danced
        the same dances in order to remain
        connected to the oldest time.

The people listened
        to birds for messages about the sky world
        and to stories of the elders in order to affirm
        the sacred wisdom of the grandfathers.

Their birthplace lay beneath their feet,
        nurturing dreams and affirmation,
uninterrupted for the time it took to create fireflies.

Whenever they danced, people renewed their

faith in rain clouds and corn.
They were consumed by
Correctness, and they never laughed at animals
for fear the animals would devour them.

People tied a rope to stars and dragged them home
for companionship.
They slid down rainbows
before they had a chance to fade
and absorbed the strength of rock
into their bones.

The drums never stopped beating,
memory never stopped throbbing,
and the heart connection went on, unbroken.

And then,
the soldiers came, and the friars
made them kneel in the dirt
to be baptized into something
incomprehensible.

Everything collapsed and ashes blew across Arenal
and the cries of the people gave sustenance
to the devouring sun.

When memory dies, the purpose of a people is obliterated.
In Arenal, the wind has claimed our lives.

OUR HEARTS WERE
ON THE GROUND

THE BEGINNING OF SICKNESS: 1590

In an old, old time
    before the white man
    gave us regulations,
    we adhered to reason.

In an old, old time
    before language was
    contaminated with noise,
    all was orderly in our village.

In those days
    we lived with Eagles and Bears.
    Our hearts were in the right place.
    We had connections to stars and moon.

When Jesus came with the pale, loud men,
    we tried to escape.
    Our lives were cut in two pieces.
    We lived in a rain of confusion.

It was the beginning of sickness.
    The beginning of debt.
    The beginning of falsehood.
    The beginning of wrecked families.
We lived with insincerity from then on.
Why should we give up our world for theirs?

Now Jesus is in our midst forever,
     like a spider spinning webs of vexation.
     Por Dios we pretend to like spiders.
     Por Dios we remember those old, old days
     of connections to Eagles and Bears.

WHEN JESUS CAME: 1590 ~ THE NAMES

They infected us with their names. Martinez. Lujan.
    Gomez.
    Names of the padres who bathed us with holy water
    to wash away our sins of innocence.

They tamed us with their names. Concha. Sanchez.
    Trujillo.
    Names of conquest meant to teach us
    the rewards of civilization.

They diluted us with their names. Montoya.
    Mondragon. Romero.
    Lujan. Concha. We sounded like them,
    names of soldiers unknown to us
    until they stole our women and drove swords
    into the hearts of our brave people.

Our names have always been dear to us.
    Lion Dreams and Dog Star. Trembling Leaf
    and Red Willow. Gray Thunder
    and Flower Pocket.

Names seared with meaning
    and the power of animals.

Our names give life to us.
>   Wind Hollow and Walking Rain. Pipe Feather
>   and Spotted Pony. Strong Elk and Eagle Wing.
>   Names
>   drawn from the bones of our beloved teachers.

These names are mirrors of our long history.
These names are what we try to become
>   as the names of our old enemies
>   suffocate our dreams.

ACOMA: 1599

In brooding, silent Acoma, thrust against the under-
belly of the sky,
        the fingers of deceit spread out and strangled
        continuity bloodlines and the right of a people
        to become wolves.

A cry of warning rose first in weary Taxio's mouth
        as Zaldivar climbed
        the steep escarpment with twelve men
        afraid of dying in a savage land.

The soldiers shivered with the audacity
        of false warriors
        as they stole two turkeys
        and pushed the maiden Cloud Heart

Into the drifted snow. Her virgin blood flowed
        across the plaza and was absorbed by her relatives.
        With tomahawks and poison arrows,
        they moved into the still, dark night,
        invisible except to stars and moon and ancestors.

Ten thousand arrows and ten thousand stones
        rained down upon the Spaniards already stiff
        with cold. The dying Zalvidar vowed
        revenge and the owls hooted

and the wind unleashed
a storm of feathers
over the earthen walls of Acoma.

Don Juan de Oñate was a man of reason,
          resplendent in velvet cape and slippers,
          his sword of possession slicing
          through pueblo resistance. He motioned
          five hundred captives to his execution court.

Miserable savages of Acoma, he said.
Pagans. Lost children of God Almighty.
What do you have to say for yourselves?
His sword gleamed like fire.

The three chieftains arose.

Caoma said: Because they stole our maize
          and flour and blankets,
          we killed them.

Xunusta said: Because they took Cloud Heart
          and destroyed her womanhood,
          we killed them.

Taxio said: Because they wished to end
          our peaceful way of life,
          we killed them.

Don Juan de Oñate said:
>For failing to surrender, for murder,
>for defiance of the noble crown of Spain
>and the holy scepter of Rome,
>I sentence you to God's own wrath
>and the judgment of kings.

For the murder of Zaldivar and his men,
>twenty years of slavery.

Warriors, step forward so I may cut off one foot
>to remind your children
>of the price of disobedience.

The warriors kept silent as Don Juan de Oñate cut off
>their feet.
>Not one man cried out.

The pile of feet gathered themselves together
>and marched away to Acoma,
>where, it is said, they keep
>the ancient village safe from harm,
>even to the present day.

THE BALANCE OF LONGEVITY

The balance of longevity was bred into our ancestors,
     who believed the past could not be destroyed
     by the shorter vision of the present.
Warriors sharpened their knives on the flinty bones
     of ancestors. Women giving birth
     buried the placenta
     to keep it from being stolen
     by the deities.

Children spoke the language of cougars and
     porcupines
     before they spoke like people.
They listened to whispers of butterfly wings,
     the complaints of grizzly bears,
     and learned their dreams from rivers.

People pulled in the horizon whenever they needed
     protection and poked a hole in the sky
     whenever they wanted to examine
     the other side of life.

They dried up the river to release the spirits of fish,
     who yearned for their home
     in the under ground lake,
     where ancestors were formed from fins and bones.

Elders devoured smoke in order to remember
        nothingness.
        Ancestors survived within a circle
        which began with a pumpkin seed
        and expanded to include the universe.

The energy released by bumblebees
        and earthworms, bird wings and the heartbeat
        of stones
        made our people invincible.
        Laughter swallowed them whole.

The drums never stopped beating.

The ancestors sang Turtle Songs to the river
        and apprehended lightning
        to make themselves
        stronger than they were before.

They captured rain clouds with fishnets
        and slid down rainbows
        before they had a chance to fade.

When the ancestors began to swerve from devotion,
        from balance, and from austerity,
        red ants grew to the size of elk
        and bore them away.

Now, they are gone. We are left to harvest

worm-eaten corn alone. Change is coming,
but is it a ripple in the water
or a convulsion of our sacred earth,
preparing to mourn our passing?

CONQUISTADORES

When the balance of longevity was destroyed,
    a void formed in the belly of the wolf
    and we fell into it, unable to remember
    the names of trees or how we flew
    with golden eagles and slammed our bravery
    against the sun.

El Rey es su gallo, said the conquistadores,
    who came to our village
    with the determination of lice.
    The king is your ruler now.

The land of your pagan ancestors
    belongs to Madre España,
    where disobedience rhymes with death.
    Locum dare. Surrender the place!

Forfeit the kinship with snails.
    Forget the wisdom of fireflies.
    Animals no longer may be worshiped
    as if they were gods.

The conquistadores tore our resistance to shreds.
    Our right to practice a natural religion was
    extinguished.
    Our bellies became as empty as gourds.

Blood ran into the dry cracks of memory.

Tears made our corn grow taller.
    Day and night, the wolf was circling our fields,
    unsatisfied.
    We yielded to his deceptive goodness,
    and were devoured.
    Spiritualis compater, said the wolf.
    I am your spiritual father.

We filled the belly of the wolf with ignorance
    and gouged his heart with madness.
    On all fours we sought to imitate his appetite,
    but our reward was greater hunger.

From the bowels of the wolf,
    we dropped through his anus
    and clutched the forgotten earth
    with fingers rubbed raw
    trying to escape confinement.

We embraced one another and worshiped the animals.
    But the wolf was always watching,
    mouth wide open to catch heathens
    such as we.

Exteri, mercatores et peregrini, we heard him say.
Foreigners, merchants, and pilgrims, unite

against the plague of insects.
Rub them out, starve them to the bone,
bleed them until dust pours from their mouths.

Facienti quidquid in se latet, Deus non denegat gratiam.
To him who does what lies within him,
God does not deny grace.

We killed the wolf before the wolf consumed our
memory.
May all our paths be fulfilled.
May the wolf devour the lamb
in order for us to know our true minds.
Agno theta. Amen.

WOMAN HEART SPIRIT

Woman heart spirit, emerging
from the exploding heat
of the universe,
why are you here among us now,
when our way of life is dying?
   I am the original wind, she said.
   I blew the Father Sun out of
   the Underworld and arranged
   the stars where I wanted them. I am
   replenishing rain,
   the essence of corn,
   the backbone
   of the sky, the beauty
   that never dies.

She gathered us into her arms and dropped us
   along the river.
   We hid ourselves in the dark
   mud houses and waited.

RAPE OF THE TEWANANGEH WOMEN: 1598

We were God's anointed horsemen, invincible as lions,
      as thirsty for women as we were for gold.
The women of Tewanangeh cowered
      like wild animals needing to hear
      God's taming voice,
      so we touched them.
They accepted our gifts
      in exchange for some of their own.
There under the screaming sun of Nueva España

We remembered our families, perola ausencia borralos
      recuerdos.
      We are God's true soldiers,
      Christians unsuited to the frontier
      to which our king remanded us,
      far from the jungle bleeding from our victories.

As the dry fields buckled under the weight of our desire,
      we prayed for deliverance
      from our abiding loneliness.

We released our manhood, obligingly.
      Querer es poder, we cried,
      certain we were invincible.

When the women of Tewanangeh began to sing,

a sea of butterflies erupted.

We all agreed.
We had to kill those butterflies
to save ourselves from shame.

LAS HUMANAS: 1668

When our metal-plated saviors arrived,
        demanding wheat and hides and corn,
        we satisfied their hunger
        as our own began.

We were slaves to misfortune,
        and while the enemy slept,
        bellies filled with wild meat,
        we were too hungry to sleep.

We dreamed of our children
        growing strong enough
        to become lions.
        Our women could not dream.
        They were turning inside out.

We were half warriors
        too weak to resist annihilation.

The coming of civilization meant our land became
        divided,
        crops were not ours to eat,
        and animals were killed without ceremony.

When we fell, the enemy cut the backbone from us.
        From our homes and fields a great wailing arose.

Our children became so dry they resembled insects.

The Thunderbird denied our prayers for rain,
  and the land contracted with the misery of conquest.

In our fields, the corn of our grandfathers withered.
In the mountains, heartsick animals departed
        before we said goodbye.
Not an animal remained as far as the eye could see.

Without food, the enemy boiled cowhides
        that once they sat upon,
        until no leather was left to eat.

In our aching village, children died first
        and we could not save them.

Women collapsed in the fields where they went
to dig for roots, their wombs hungry for babies.

Our shattered warriors fell upon the earth
        and embraced its emptiness.
The lament for lost families rose to the sky place
        where corn stalks still sang of rain
        and worms waited to become butterflies.

The voices of our ancestors rose on the dust:
        Strangers have stolen your land,

your homes, your bodies.
But your hearts are strong. Wait and see.

Five hundred corpses turned over where they had fallen
and pulled themselves up
until at last they faced the horizon.
Come, they said. We know where plenty is.

The people marched eastward to the buffalo prairie,
where they convinced those creatures
to come home with them
so they would never starve again.

SLAVERY

We as children have a right
to live without fear. We are
the smallest people, born into the world
without hatred or misconception. Our
enemies tore us away from our mothers
to trade for horses. We will never see
our village again.

We don't look back as we walk the rocky path,
tied together with a rope,
with nothing in our bellies
and nothing in our minds.

But look, there is a raven flying overhead
and small blue flowers growing at our feet.
There is the wind, which carries us back
to the place where our memories began.

Now, let us sing.

SONG FOR A NEWBORN PAST

A little while we lived along the river, not forever here,
although we were entrusted with forever
by our ancestors, who comforted us
when our hearts were on the ground.

We lived surrounded by the earth
on six sides, but the earth helped no one
when we departed from our obligations
and became imitations of our former selves.

Our people arrived in harmony, and they left
with an oath to survive destruction
of a future that had no edge.
In our dreams, we saw rivers consumed
by fire and forests defiled by greed.

Our ancestors, rising from false memory, offered
allegiance to the world of mystery,
and we, considering the alternatives,
accepted.

HOW A PEOPLE REVOLTED

PUEBLO COURAGE

Into the place where the eagle was resting,
    we went. Into the rock where the river
    was forming, we went. Into the earth
    where old bones were decaying, we went.

Into the star trails, we went. Along
    the bottoms of oceans, we went. New lives
    formed out of rock and water, and these we took

To make our weak blood strong. We created
    an invisible world to satisfy a visible need.
    In our persistence we created fire
    out of nothingness.

From the ashes of our old life
    a different kind of flame arose.

DESTINY

Up among the clouds, the ancestors are weeping on
behalf of people deprived of ritual. The violation
of women meant that our unborn children were
denied the rich blood

Of coyotes, antelope, and bears. The destruction of
our ways began amidst the battle to maintain
dinity. Our warriors died defending our right
to continue as allies of the sun, but our enemies
saw them as obstacles to progress, so they
killed them.

Believing that our courage would save us,
we watched a river of blood
wash over our emaciated land.

We did not believe their ways,
but we embraced them
in order to survive.

As our villages fell,
our prayers sustained us.

WE BECAME AS MOUNTAINS

Out of the pain of uncertainty,
      slavery,
      and the rupture of a common future,
We became as mountains,
      strong and unchanged.
      Nothing could touch us anymore.

Rivers and rocks became our allies.
      The four-legged creatures
      connected us to their wisdom.

We became as mountains,
      forged by ice and wind,
      adversity and hopelessness.

The spirit of our ancestors filled
      our bellies, and soon
      our hunger disappeared.

WAITING: 1675

Beneath the hallowed ruins of our village
  lie the legends of eagles
   merging with the tenacity of stones.

Fish have secrets so deep
   they only share them with rivers
   possessing the courage to move on.
We are one with patience.
   We honor a clear memory
   that plunders our desire to forget.

Our blood drips with the pain of exploitation.
Our bodies are covered with the dirt of conquest.
Let us fling ourselves in the river.

Wait. Our stories are anxious to be heard now
   when we hold between our hands
   the weapons we will need
   to drive the invaders from our homes.

POPÉ'S REVOLT: 1680

All across the ravaged land that seethes inside my
      memory,
      the villages are filled with unrest,
      dead smoke, and
      the breath of fat padres.

Otermin's flags of yellow silk flutter
      and obedience is demanded
      along with all our food.

We will kill them, I say,
      and begin to steal their horses
      while they are sleeping.

Deep in a kiva of Braba, the spirits called
      Cavdi, Tilini, and Tleume
      instruct me in warfare.

We begin to steal their weapons,
      And in the dirt,
      I draw a map of where they are.

Rising on the wind of Four Directions,
      fanned by the anger of a wounded people,
      Catiti and I dream of power greater than theirs.

Never again will our people be humiliated
        nor will a false religion
        be imposed upon us.

From Braba, the runners and their knotted yucca cords
        fan out through the cactus and the piñons,
        across sharp rocks and deep rivers
        where fish help them across.
        Faster, I cry.

I am their king and many of the chieftains hate me.
        We will kill them, too, if they do not obey me.
        The ways of the enemy are creeping in.

Suscipiat Dominus sacrificium, I sing,
        May the Lord receive your sacrifice.
        The God-words of the padres choke me
        with their righteousness.

I cut the baptism from my person
        and stab the priest until his blood flows out.
        Many padres died that day,
        the words of their holy faith
        frozen upon their lips.

Kill them, I said to the warriors.
        Kill them in memory of generations
        who perished here. Kill them.

Forgive me. I see the Blessed Virgin,
      whose kindly face I smashed myself.
      I see it all,
      and now I cannot sleep.
Am I to be damned for saving my people?

Get me a chariot so I can ride like a king.
      Make me a crown of fir branches
      and kinnikinnick.
      It's all that will save me now.

My hands are drenched in blood.
      No one thanks me for my courage.

Popé is nothing now. But the oppressed are free.
They are living inside the Palace of the Governors
      with their animals. The enemy attacks.
      The people fight among themselves.

           What am I to do?

LAST SURVIVORS, CIQUIQUE: 1837

The people of Ciquique were made
    of the fiber of trees,
    the muscle of bears,
    the blood of cougars.

They were part of earth and sky and water,
    yet they were also children
    of women able to see
    inside the hearts of stones.

The sacred rhythm created by the sleeping earth,
    wings, and wind
    made people seem invincible
    for a hundred generations.

Laughter rolled out from the walls,
    and people made love in daylight, unashamed.
Grandfather drums never stopped beating.
    People sang to the river
    to keep it alive.
When the invaders arrived,
    bringing rules to their happy lives,
    the people resisted.

The friars beat into their minds
    the unyielding dogma

of sixteen centuries,
which meant no more nakedness
and no more dances with animals.

When sickness began at Ciquique, the Corn Mothers
abandoned their responsibilities.
People died without songs of farewell.

The chieftains prayed for release from indignity.
On the wind rose stories
told by grandmothers desperate
for gentleness to be remembered.

Grandfather drums were silenced, and in the kivas,
the sacred snake that had protected them
crawled away and was never seen again.

At last only seventeen people remained,
shards of a past that had deserted them.

In tattered moccasins, they walked.
In sorrow, they walked.
In uncertainty, they walked.
Step by step, they began to awaken.

They sang the old songs and beat the old drum.
Laughter and dancing resumed.
In a village called Jemez,

they became new people.

But their hearts remained at Ciquique,
where red dust devoured
the outlines of their memory.

FULL CIRCLE

TAOS: 1847

Bright flowers of destruction bloomed that winter
        amidst wooden markers impaled on the
        bloody earth
        of Taos, encouraged by songs echoing across
        a nurturing sky of memory.

Two earth mounds wet with tears of rebellion
        lay side by side
        in the shadow of the ruined church
        into which Montojo had led his people,
        believing Christian soldiers
        to be inclined toward mercy.

The church collapsed from the weight of so much agony,
        walls perforated by cannon balls.
        The sacred village began to melt
        from the smoldering heat of battle

Two little girls ran out into the smoke before the eyes
        Of eight hundred soldiers anxious to
        dispense justice reinforced by weapons.
Oh, you little ones!
Get out of the line of fire!

Two Skies Together and Moon Dancer were sisters,
        one dark, the other lighter.

They were the laughing daughters
of desert and mountain,
children of Spanish vecinos
and a Taos woman called Tree.
They shared the same dark root
of generation and lack of expectation.

Smoke settled over the plaza like a shroud,
and the soldiers said later,
they did not see the girls.
They thought they were dogs.

Two Skies died first, clinging
to a statue of la Madre de Dios,
hoping it would save her from the bayonet
that pierced her belly.

Moon Dancer hid behind the burning altar on her knees.
She felt only a warm, deep river
of blood surging from her mouth,
and then she heard the crack of rifles.

She prayed for Salt Woman to save her,
for songs to fill her emptiness,
but all she heard were the cries of her people,
dying from their misfortune.

On those two earth mounds, the mother called Tree
left red flowers for her daughters.

They were magical flowers.
Whenever people looked at them,
they turned into birds or butterflies.

Even to the present day red flowers bloom in winter
at the Pueblo of Taos. And two small girls can
be seen
running across the plaza.

They are laughing.

ATOMIC CITY: 1945

On the parched tongue of the southwest wind they come,
    brave Ohuwa and Kawo, warriors beheaded
    by Oñate and Otermin,
    who saw them as obstacles to authority.

Women sing the ancient songs of Corn and Deer
    in order to feel connection between
    those warriors and the lasting gifts of seasons.

On the mesas, our friends are drops of disappearing water,
    Agoyo and Tyugha, holy men blinded by
    deception.
    Their lost children are with them,
    armed with pumpkins and corn tassels,
    but they are reduced to skeletons.

Women dance like corpses, remembering the blood
    that congeals their history into scabs of misfortune.
    On the dust they ride as specks of flying red earth,
    Pauna and Fana, our hanged elders.

Alive with news of bumblebees, we open our ears
    to stories of ancestors still breathing truths.
    The enemy must bend in order to be useful,
    and we must have patience when we are starving.

We will kill them with our courage,
    shame them with our pride.
    They will fall from too much food.

On forked lightning they strike, Po-towa and Kuya-towa,
    our murdered leaders, with heat enough to melt
    the obsession of our enemies.

They are here with animosity, with impatience,
    with twenty million slaughtered
    natives no longer in a position of respect.
    They are here to commiserate
    with the sorrowing earth split open.

Green fields tilled by loving hands
    are filled with poison ash. Birds die.

Mad men are building ghastly weapons of destruction
    in the hills where we used to dance
    and where the spirit of our ancestors still lives.

Men who embrace destruction are poor in spirit.
They will not see God, either.

FULL CIRCLE

Some say the world is dying,
but I don't believe them.
There is always something good to see.

My ancestors would not have given up.
I, in my modern house, cannot give up either.
To give up is to die.

My voice goes on
and I fight like a warrior for
creatures who cannot speak.
The voices of turtles and falcons are within me,
and I must put myself in Brother Bear's skin.

The end is the beginning. The full circle
of my life is nothing more
than one footstep going on.